HELLO, FISH!

VISITING THE CORAL REEF

by Sylvia A. Earle

with photographs by Wolcott Henry

SCHOLASTIC INC.

New York Toronto London Auckland Sydney
Mexico City New Delhi Hong Kong Buenos Aires

For the fish,
for all who wish fish well,
for Wolcott, and for two fish-watchers to be:
Deirdra Henry McKelvy and Taylor Earle Griffith
— Sylvia Earle

To Sylvia and Angel,
for your inspiration and support,
and to the next generation of those dedicated to exploring
and protecting the marine world
— Wolcott Henry

ISBN 0-439-18816-4

Published by Scholastic Inc., 557 Broadway, New York, NY 10012,
by arrangement with the National Geographic Society.

12 11 10 9 8 7 6 5 4 3 2 2 3 4 5 6 7/0

Printed in the U.S.A. 24

First Scholastic printing, March 2002

Book design by Patrick Collins

Special thanks to Paul Humann for fish identification,
to Carl Mehler, Director of Maps, Book Division,
and to Michelle H. Picard, Map Production

Front cover: Clownfish in an anemone
Back cover: Yellowtail snapper watch Sylvia Earle read a book about fish.
Title page: Yellow blenny

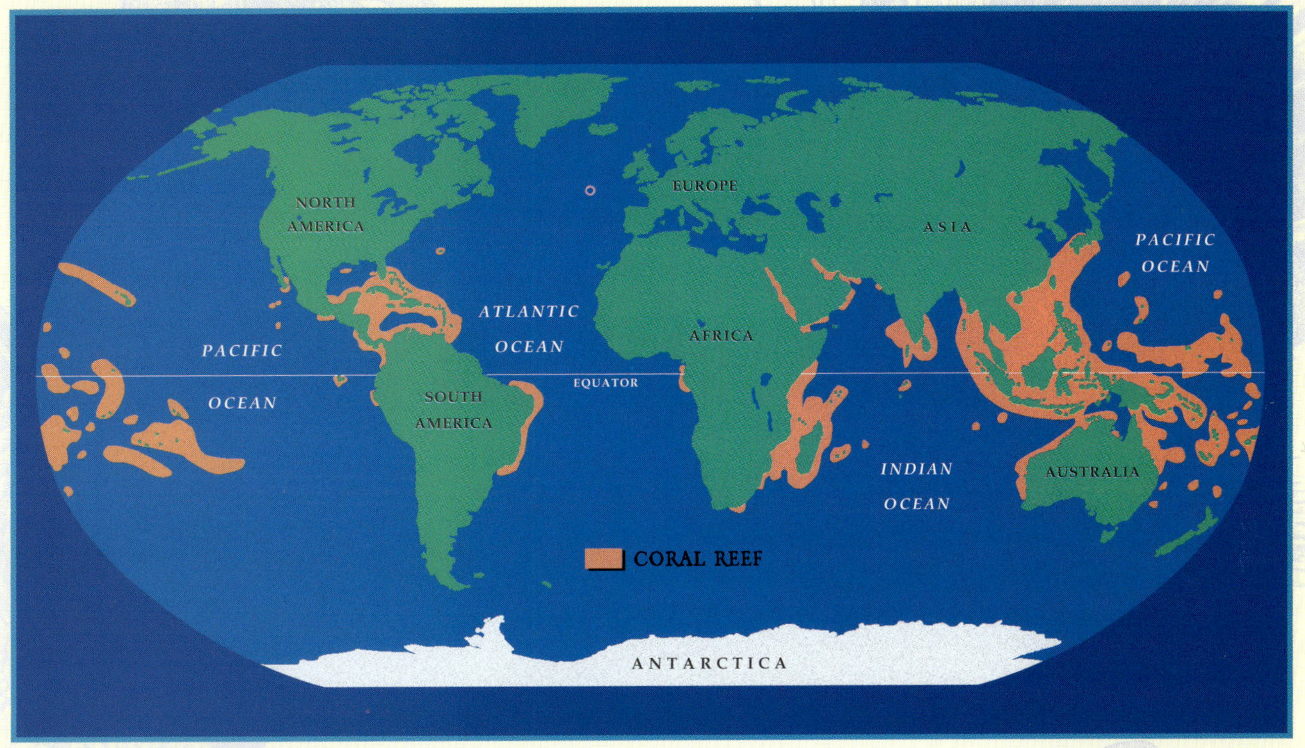

Of all the kinds of creatures that have backbones—people, frogs, snakes, and birds to name a few—fish are the most numerous. They have gills to help them breathe, scales to protect their skin, and fins for swimming through the waters of the world. All of the fish in this book live in and around coral reefs. These rocklike structures, which take millions of years to form, are made up of billions of skeletons from tiny animals called corals. These reefs, shown in orange on the map, flourish in shallow areas of warm ocean waters. You will discover, as you read this book, that reef fish come in a variety of shapes, colors, and sizes. Each has its own special place in the wondrous world of the coral reef.

IF YOU WONDER WHAT FISH DO ALL DAY
AND HOW THEY SPEND THEIR NIGHTS,
COME GLIDE WITH ME INTO THE SEA.
WE'LL SAY HELLO TO CREATURES WHO
MAKE THEIR HOME IN A REALM OF BLUE.

Spotted Moray

I often stop and play with morays.
I've even hugged a few!

Moray eels can be dangerous, though,
if you happen to be a small fish or octopus.
Watch out!
You could become an eel meal!
But people aren't on their menu.
In fact, these gentle and curious fish
remind me of kittens.
It's easy to see why this one
is called a spotted moray,
a fine name for a totally freckled fish.

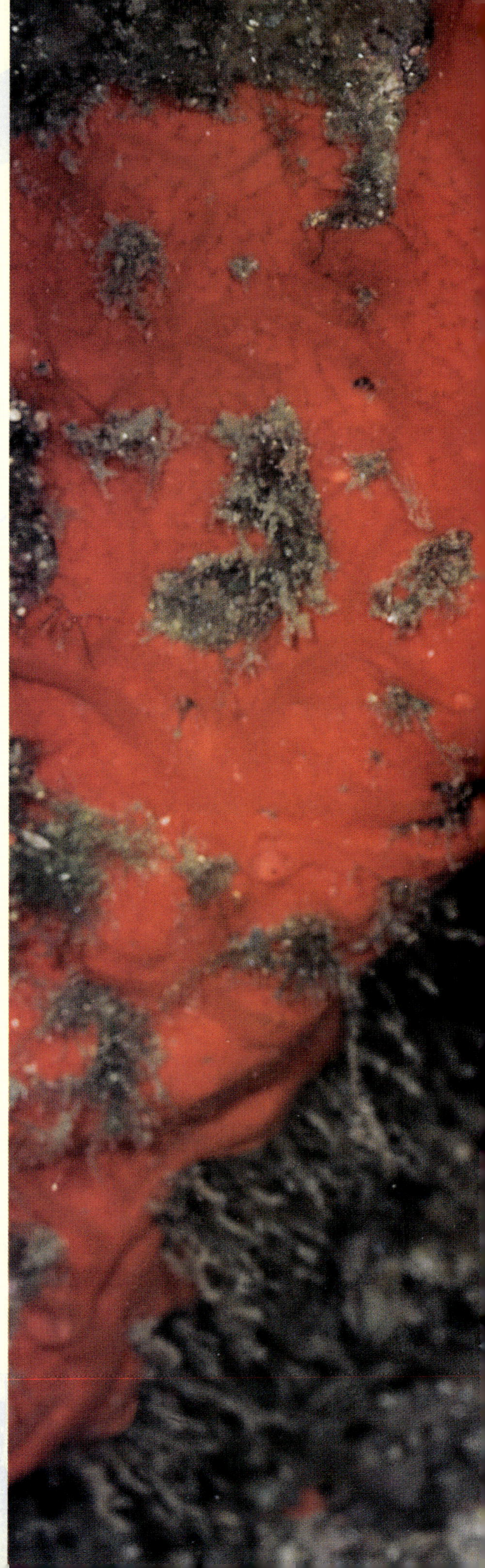

Clownfish

In an anemone's soft, slippery arms
A clownfish hides as large fish pass by.

It looks as though this fish
might be in trouble
among the stinging tentacles
of a sea anemone. But no!
This is a clownfish,
one of dozens of kinds of small fish
that actually make their homes
and raise their families
in places that are deadly to other creatures.
Clownfish coat their fins and scales
with a wonderful kind of slimy goo
that keeps them from being stung.

STARGAZER

Now you see it, now you don't.
Is it a pile of pebbles and sand, or a fish?

With clever camouflage
stargazers fool big fish that might want to eat them.
They also trick the little fish they want to eat.
When something tasty swims by,
that big, toothy mouth quickly opens
and gulps down a meal.
With eyes that always look up,
it's easy to see why these fish are called stargazers.
But, since they live in the sea,
maybe they should be called starfish gazers!

SILVERTIP SHARK

A silver swimmer in the reef, this shark
Is one of the ancient ocean dwellers.

If you could go back in time
300 million years,
you would find no whales,
no dolphins, no seals,
no dinosaurs, no birds,
or trees or flowers or frogs.
But there would be sharks in the sea.
Many people are afraid of sharks,
but of the more than 350 kinds now known,
very few ever even nibble on us.
People kill so many sharks, though,
that some kinds may soon be gone forever.
Let's take care so the sea can always be
home to sharks.

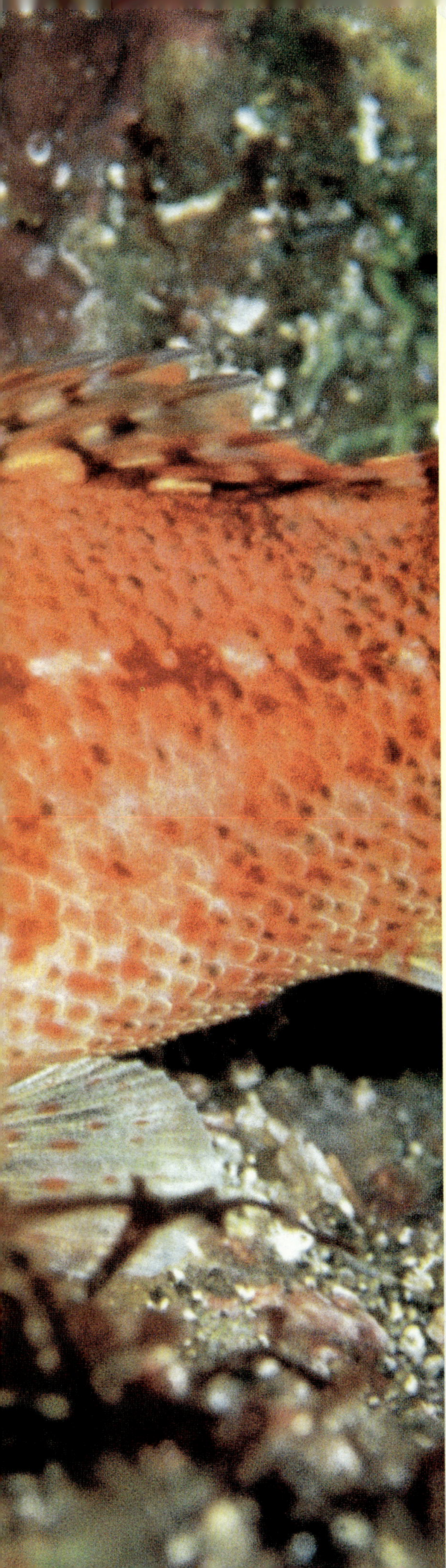

RAINBOW SCORPIONFISH

Hovering still against the reef,
A scorpionfish hides.

You might think that a red fish
would be easy to find in a blue ocean.
But against colorful sponges and corals,
this scorpionfish blends right in.
His spiny fins are a good defense,
but if you don't hurt him,
he won't hurt you.
His large, beautiful eyes
help him find his way around in the sea.
While I watch him, he watches me.

Brown Goby

Look closely to find little gobies,
Like this one peeking out at you.

This brown goby
may venture out a short distance
from his adopted home,
an empty worm tube.
But at the first hint of danger,
he'll dive back into shelter for safety.
Like most gobies,
this one props himself up
on the small fins under his chin
when he wants to look out
at the world.

DAMSELFISH

This jewel-like creature with
Blue-and-gold eyes is a damselfish.

It is one in a family
of hundreds of creatures
most commonly found in tropical seas
around coral reefs.
Most are no bigger than your hand,
but inside that sheath of sleek scales
is a very tough fish.
When provoked, damselfish
will chase away creatures
many times their size—
even me!

Red Goby

This red goby has a sweeping tail
And on its back a ruby sail!

I sometimes find these fish
with a magnifying glass.
Can you imagine that within a body
no bigger than your little finger
there can be teeth and eyes
and a backbone, stomach, heart, and tongue,
and all the other things fish need to live?
Gobies eat tiny shrimplike creatures.
Most spend their time in a small area
and can live for years in a single shell.

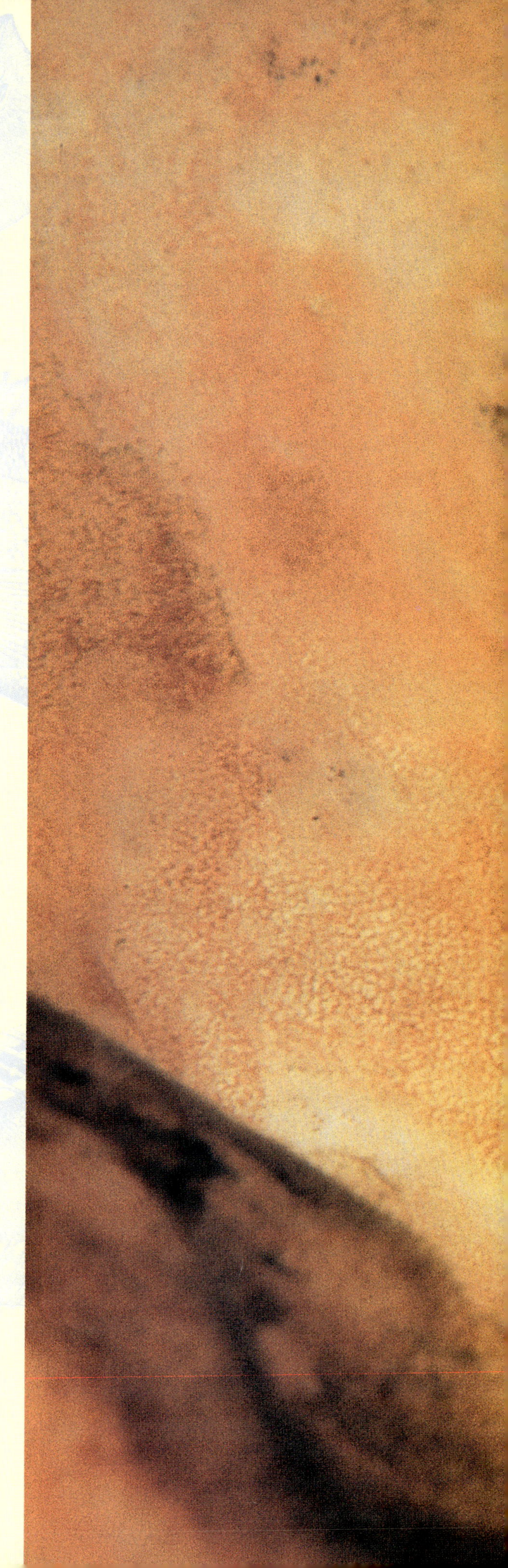

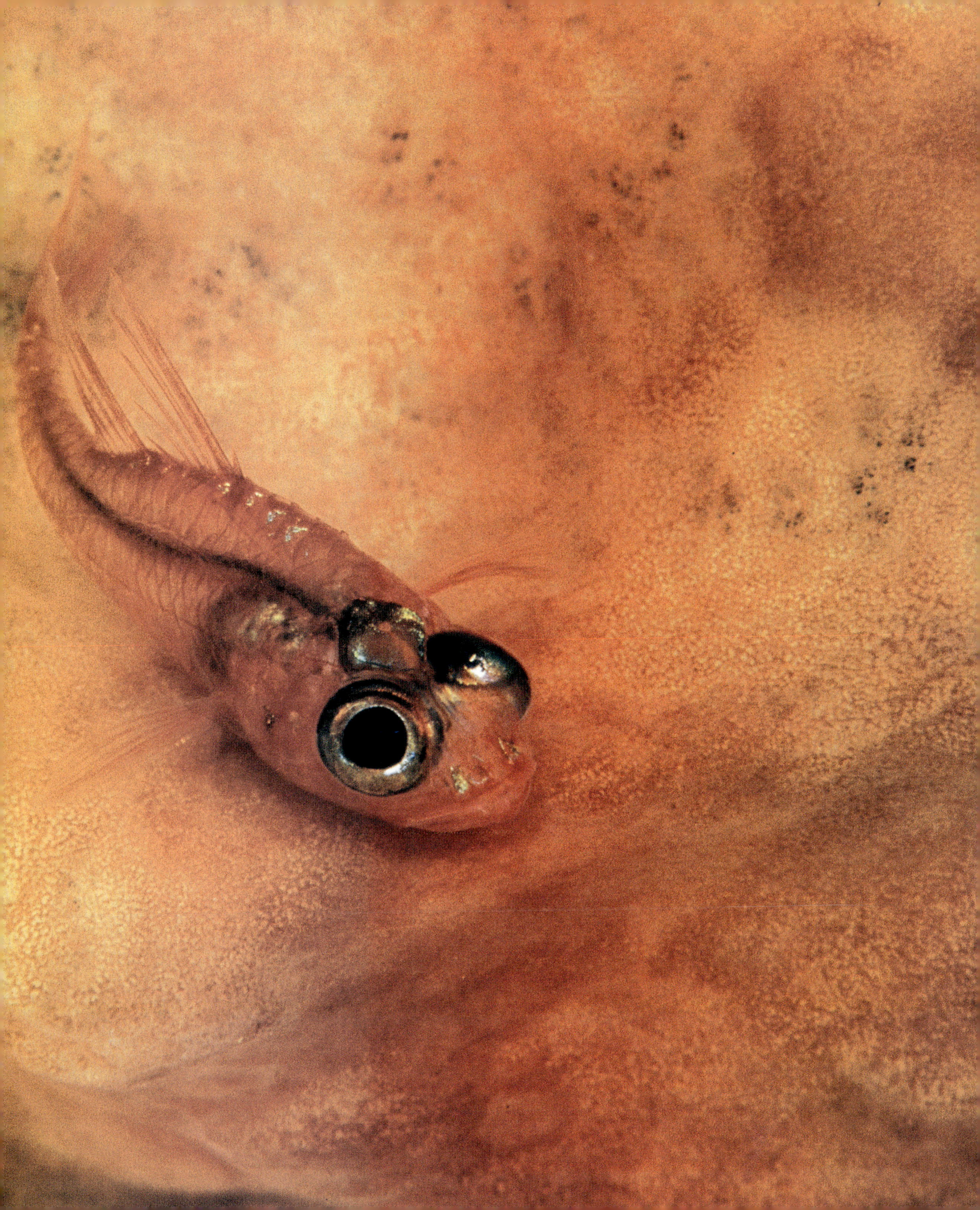

Striped Catfish

Cats aren't the only creatures
Famous for their whiskers!

Catfish whiskers are soft and sensitive—
very useful feelers, especially in the dark.
There are hundreds of kinds of catfish
in the ocean and in some lakes,
rivers, and streams.
None have scales—quite unusual for fish!
None have fur, either, of course.
But all have gills like other fish.
Little catfish tend to stay together.
Probably they're safer than they would be
if each one swam around the reef alone.

Frogfish

With bulbous eyes and slippery skin,
This must be the well-named frogfish!

Actually, all frogs and all of the 20,000 or so kinds of fish
and all of the 9,000 kinds of birds
and all of the thousands of kinds of mammals
and all turtles and lizards and snakes have something in common.
We all have backbones—vertebrae—
unlike most of the rest of life on Earth.
Beetles don't, crabs don't, starfish don't, octopuses don't,
nor do jellyfish, of course!
But frogs and fish and people everywhere do—
including you!

Spotted Stingray

Graceful, gentle creatures, rays glide
Through the sea like giant butterflies.

Spotted stingrays pause now and then
to dine on clams, snails, and other
small animals that live in soft sand or mud
on the seafloor.
Many kinds of rays and
their toothy relatives—the sharks—
live in the oceans of the world.
Millions of years ago
rays and sharks were swimming
in the deep sea.
And, they still are!

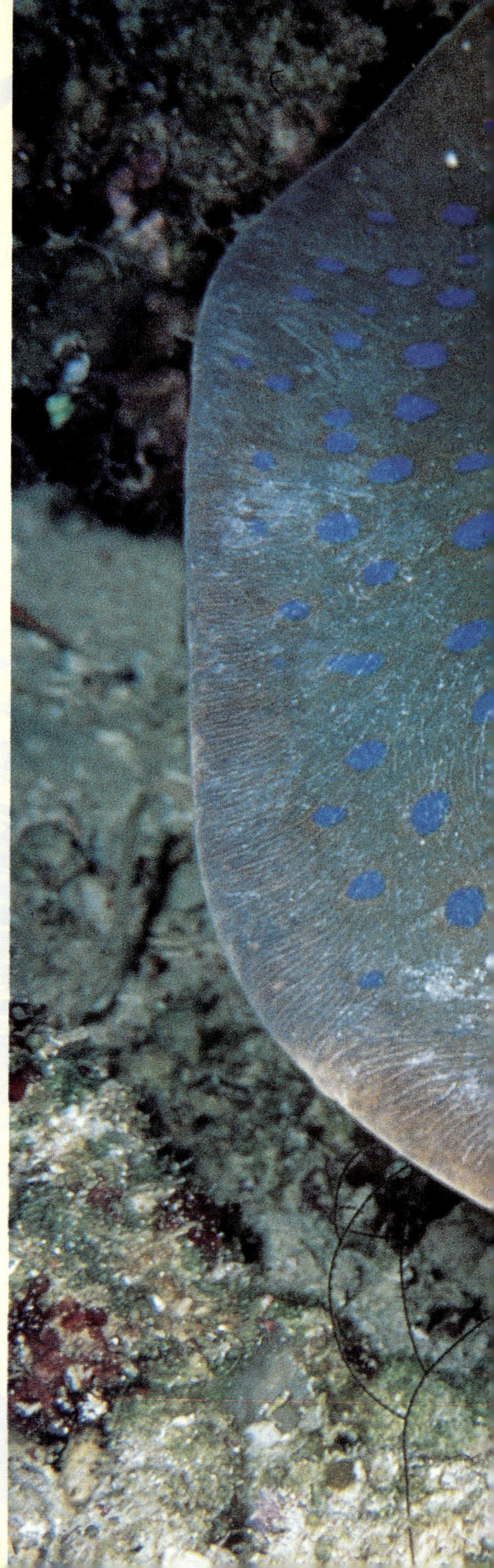

SEAHORSE

This curvy fish—what could it be?
A seahorse, with room to roam the sea.

Seahorses are small fish with large eyes.

They have a big appetite for tiny crustaceans.

Like people, they choose partners for life.

They usually stay together, even during stormy weather.

Seahorse mothers lay their eggs in special pouches

that seahorse fathers have in their bellies.

Weeks later, fully formed little fish

swim out of the pouches into the sea—

ready to grow up

and find partners of their own.

Great Barracuda

Red Lizardfish

Scrawled Cowfish

Queen Angelfish

School of Silversides

Now that you've met a few of my friends, I hope you'll learn more about the sea where they live.

Leopard Blenny

Queen Parrotfish

Spanish Hogfish

Sylvia A. Earle

Sylvia Earle is a marine biologist, author, lecturer, and ocean explorer. She is the National Geographic Society's Explorer-in-Residence for 1998 and 1999. As part of the Sustainable Seas Expeditions launched in 1998 with Society support, Earle plans to dive in all 12 U.S. marine sanctuaries. Called "Her Deepness" by the *New York Times*, Sylvia Earle has a B.S. from Florida State University and a Ph.D. from Duke University, as well as numerous honorary doctorates. When not underwater, Sylvia Earle lives in Oakland, California.

NATALIE FOBES

Wolcott Henry

Wolcott Henry is an underwater photographer who has explored coral reef areas all over the world, including Indonesia, Papua New Guinea, the Galápagos Islands, Hawaii, and the Florida Keys. He is president of the Curtis and Edith Munson Foundation, an organization that supports marine conservation in North America. Henry's photographs are often used by nonprofit groups to communicate the importance of coral reefs. He lives in Washington, D.C.